Loans a
not ret
at the
3 time
Please

W0010099

HG

Porter

The Cos... ...sness (1978; reissued 1987)
Fast Forward (1984)
The Automatic Oracle (1987)
Collected Poems (1983; reissued 1988)
A Porter Selected (1989)

POSSIBLE WORLDS

Peter Porter

Oxford   Melbourne

OXFORD UNIVERSITY PRESS

1989

Oxford University Press, Walton Street, Oxford OX2 6DP
Oxford New York Toronto
Delhi Bombay Calcutta Madras Karachi
Petaling Jaya Singapore Hong Kong Tokyo
Nairobi Dar es Salaam Cape Town
Melbourne Auckland
and associated companies in
Berlin Ibadan

Oxford is a trade mark of Oxford University Press

British Library Cataloguing in Publication Data
Porter, Peter
Possible worlds
I. Title
821
ISBN 0-19-282660-3

Library of Congress Cataloging in Publication Data
Porter, Peter.
Possible worlds / Peter Porter.
p. cm.
I. Title.
PR9619.3.P57P67 1989
821—dc19 89-3057
ISBN 0-19-282660-3 (pbk.)

Typeset by Wyvern Typesetting Ltd
Printed in Great Britain by
J. W. Arrowsmith Ltd, Bristol

For Gavin Ewart

ACKNOWLEDGEMENTS

Acknowledgements are due to the editors of the following periodicals in which some of these poems first appeared: *The Adelaide Review, The Age, Ambit, Antaeus, Descant, The Listener, London Magazine, London Review of Books, Meanjin, The New Welsh Review, Poetry Business, Poetry Chicago, Quadrant, Scripsi, Strawberry Fair, Thames Poetry, Times Literary Supplement, Westerly, ZLR*. Two poems are included in the Festschrift for Raymond Tschumi (Hochschule, St Gallen, Switzerland). Other poems were broadcast in programmes of the ABC and BBC.

CONTENTS

The trumpet cries
This is the successor of the invisible.

This is its substitute in stratagems
Of the spirit. This, in sight and memory,
Must take its place, as what is possible
Replaces what is not.

WALLACE STEVENS, 'Credences of Summer'

NEXT TO NOTHING

The casque of a dragon-fly
eaten out by ants
is living etherialized,
bone round the library
of the brain—
　　　　　One day
when digging in the sand
for pippis I looked about
and saw beyond the beach
a mountain of their shells
a century old
where aborigines
used to come to feast.
One shell is next to nothing
in the dark of being born,
so I dropped it in the bucket
knowing I must offer Heaven
the softer part of me,
my contentious mind,
and leave behind another shell
on the unthinking shore
of the authorial continent.

A PHYSICAL WORLD

To have sat in the awkwardest tree
playing cubby-houses and to be the one
who had to beg his friends to find him
a girl to take to the holiday dance.

To sight the bright bees of ambition buzzing
in a book while the unimprovable sun
blazed down on sumptuous emptiness
and asphalt melted into mediocrity.

So many dead, there was this wealth only
in the family, that you invented the blaze
of extinction: to be such a virtuoso
of yourself that truth remained untellable.

The great world still sitting in trees or looming
over your head in crawling buses—
strange to have no way of touching animals
or comforting a crying face at nightfall.

How ridiculous to be Columbus
offering Isabella the earliest gold of America
when you could be Da Ponte giving Mozart
his first sight of the libretto of *Figaro*.

DECUS ET TUTAMEN

Come with me to vistas of a low dissolving bay
Where mud, fine shingle and the mangrove's toppling roots
Run up to golfing grass, the humpy haciendas of
Unromantic people stretched along a wire of happiness
From self-made history to a climatized inane.
In the tourist season so much shit from the hotels
Enters these discipled waters that the birds fly off,
Though fish increase. Ecology is shit, says the white-shooed
Magnate in his barbican of glass; the universe is stable,
The sewers of LA can take a furlough, what is
A littoral of winding tides upon a fret of mud
If not a model sewage farm? The trouble with the world
Is that it can't be turned to money. We live on a bank note:
The coins are in our bones, their galaxies extend
Through dreams 'to the round earth's imagined corners',
And we still sleep Columbus's sleep, happy to know
The keel will drag upon another slave-worked shore,
An economy of viral flu and feathers.
Praise our intrepid fathers who left swards of stinking geese,
The clog-tympanum streets beneath progressive lighting
(A Rippered dawning of good dividends) to fetch
The future to a sleeping coast. Unpack the corded bales,
You practical romantics, you have a century
Of mercantile weekends before the Tyrian traders come,
The ethnic restaurants and dressing for the theatre.
Meanwhile, exhaustion of newcomers takes its toll:
The flogging martinet no sooner dead than makes a ghost
To ride the river bank beneath the stars' eye-holes,
The heavens a gaol for Lancashire lapsarians
And God on watch. But comes the long-believed relief
As sure as Scottish pipes or camel convoys through the night—
We all can dream ourselves inside Free Trade,
We dip our fingers in the stoup of cash, we bless
The house with pictures of great pioneers on banknotes—
So beautiful is money, it is the nation in low carving,
The miracles by St Democracy among
The bargain car-lots, the blue rinse hyper-rise,
Selling short the wimps and setting up sons of the Manse
As Neo-Emperors. Turn the small disc in your hand,
The coin, the CD of desire; it proves its plastic cousins
Men of substance, it makes the whale-sounds appropriate

3

To conservationists of the TV twilight,
It sings across all latitudes. Now, on sunny afternoons,
Our yachts at anchor, their cordless phones asleep,
We see ourselves the ancient tribesmen of the land
Telling snake legends to the rainbow trees,
Reverted like the glasshouse hills and mortared gullies
To pure landscape till our very death becomes
A record in a rock, perfection of the will to live.

WOOP WOOP

The backtrack Trebizond of everyone,
it is in a disc of starfish where the lakes
are Balatons and the muslin-valenced ladies
bring library books to town as if it were
no more than six weeks since their husbands died.

Here start the open-shirted young sophisticates
whose fathers took the franchise for a new
variety of Cola, the ones whose poems and whose
gossip-columns are made the more intelligently
decadent by their need to tame the capital.

Out of its famished acres come anecdotes
of men with recipes for 'cockatoo-au-vin',
of fossickers in muddy dams taming Irish tunes
on one-string fiddles—rumours started here
sell beer ten thousand miles from 'Truth To Tell'.

Juggernauts are planned to pass this very place
when six-lane highways from the Bi-Centenary
stride beside the hoardings, but the point
of all this opening-up must be our doubt
that such a site will stay to welcome us.

Although an ancient and austere referent
it is younger than the harboured megalopolis
it backs, since every journey to simplicity
is inland and the parrots dress in ever-brighter
greens and scarlets the emptier the lakes they lap.

The movie industry could not exist without it:
wasp-waisted girls are seen riding after Schumann
to the soup-tin letter-box to hear that London
wants their novels, and following riots in Europe,
amuse their company just naming its odd name.

Perhaps it has no future; we know already,
despite remoteness and the different sorts of fly,
it has suburban aspects: nobody here must wait
a day to hire his favourite video, and one of its sons
read 'The Death of Virgil' through his Sunday School.

It is full of details we agree to love—
the cat called Fortunata, the minestrone
made in milk-churns, an aunt who mounted 'Tosca'
in a shearing shed: outside town, it offers you
the peace inside your mother's mind, the need to get away.

RIVER RUN

There is no source, though something like a bird
distances the very distance in its hoverings
and, tugging at a twig, will mark the start.

Out of nowhere to a little gully, the bits of life
like startings-up of always crying ground
gather and roll forward to a pool.

A pool, a pearl, another pearl, a pool—
the river is arriving where the dew
dries on the early paperbarks as dust.

Every childhood has its playground kills,
the innocentest cruelty and the wet
despair which no maturer pain can quell.

A time of waterfalls, of leaps round rocks
that flash their dignity, a use for history—
our fathers went down this peculiar road.

Where the gorges start, our planners stipulate
well-fenced lookouts and well-hung flowers,
blood smears of bottlebrush and banksia.

Hard-working days of green ambition,
the river and the self are broadening
among short-lived crimes, a gaudy flap of parrots.

As suddenly as afternoon the surge becomes
a modified achievement—where love has stalled,
the four-wheel-drives churn up a path of frogs.

Crops on the shore, a dog asleep upon a cushion
and the arbour heavy with the scent of lily—
out there the water-skiers skim the farther bank.

Wide as a yawn, the slow-coach river now
bastes in itself and boils the leaves
upon its surface: it is going home.

Alluvial plains of age and aspiration
needing great engineering works and
pumping stations—the doctor checks its heart.

Is this the run-up to the Third Millennium
or a ghostly dock of dreams? Each night
we take a boat upon a different thread of delta.

There in the dark, a little distance off,
the breakage sound of ocean—we will dream here
and hope never to reach the pounding Heads.

Instead, make home and common cause
with fish heads and the floating debris
of the wharfs. The river has no start,

How could it bring us to a proper end?

THE BLAZING BIRDS

With their wicker worry wok of claque and claim
the birds play Scrabble on the air. Sky is stretched
and naked nightmare's strung on fencing wire.

On a mat of pier, Australia's noisy birds
are sucking anthems. So much suck comes out
with lumps of sun it spells Magnificat.

Certainly it's a privilege to get up drunk
and leave a note—I'm not inside my ears, I'm
parleying with certain parrots of importance.

All at once and always changing gear
the Sistine servers shrike. Perennial
the praise and every liturgy a laugh.

Telephones are ringing on the wire
but men are starved of epithets. Boiled words,
the birds say, are as close as you will get.

The tirra-lirra parliament sits on.
'Ugly old man with crocheted wobbly hair,
you're wong, you're wong, your curry's doubly wong.'

Give them an inch and they'll take a worm.
A team of locusts trains beside the Firsts,
black cockatoos above a stand of fire.

I almost lose my way among similitudes.
Bird cries may seam into our symphonies
but in this garden only spiders spin.

The 'twenty-eight', the spangled drongo, kooka
with its caco-credo, magpie mutts,
what messages they drag across the sky!

Kings to fish for, larks to scent the air,
a parlement of fowles refuelling,
and Bib and Bub expelled from Paradise.

THE ECSTASY OF ESTUARIES

It is the right time to come here visiting,
Where villagers saved suicidal whales
And sand is constituted white
Beneath blue hulls—a time of times
Precluding death and constantly ahead
Of madness. Rest here, that have no absolute.

What might rock sleep is breaking out at sea
On reefs which bear the Southern Ocean;
Up-river pelicans on posts applaud
Such widening to island esplanades,
A shallow onus of the tide, the whiting
Sketching on the bottom their own shapes.

Nothing is curable but may still be endured.
Voices wait near water for career,
The karri are as various as signatures
And people out of cars confess they find
A fantasy in being what they are,
Slaves to the ancient brightness of the sea.

A magistracy of memory condemns:
Give us your childhood reminiscences,
Fan us awake with scholarship—was that
The famous Ardath pack, the Sydney Silkie's bark,
Were we the partners of those afternoons
Which lounged about in bamboo concert-rooms?

Staunchness of land slipping into light,
Of sandbanks drying from the ebbing tide,
Opens a thinking principality—
It's always a thousand miles from where to where
And will be Sunday by the railway clock,
Apprenticeship to dying in the dark.

To scatter toast crumbs to the gulping gulls
And let the dinghy flutter on the tide,
To be reliving what was hardly lived
When years ago the boat came back at dusk,
A father and a son, strange strangers, home,
This is the storytelling of the blood.

A countryside of changes still unchanged
Where no '*vielleicht*' will travel as 'perhaps',
Remorseless movement that a wayward tune
Has challenged into permanency,
This ecstasy of estuaries prepares
A tableland for time to wander in.

THE WIND AT BUNDANON

In the code of invisible painting
trees are pushing colour to its limit,
a green which parses understanding.

This wind has broken free from minds.
It is assured by sites and measurements,
by the coral trees' red rip-tide
and washing blazing on the line.
The bunya pines' high installation
is a clash of gears and by the lake
the servant oranges are silvering
a black estate.

The wind can't see what we can see.
It is invisible opacity
and slams the shutters on a rising cake.
Cockatoos on a tea-towel
hear it at the window and fear for
their active squadrons in the field.
Its cousin fire
flicks a Draculine antenna from the grate—
the Master's come in glowing granulars.

This merciless blowing has to be
a metaphor of something. The teeth
of this land are worn to stumps but look
at what a gummy grannying can do.
From the river's haunting-point
wind sweeps away stale helicopters,
laggard cloud, complacent quietness.
Taller clouds stand back from barricades:
let Pentecost amaze the visitors,
sky and the four-inch grass are history.

The wind has learned communication's lesson,
these days it rides about on four-wheel drive.
Knowing the public for anthologies,
it asks us to invent comparisons,
but don't ascribe its billowing likenesses
to marketing gone crazy; there was a wrench
when complaining and perfectible mankind

came to Australia. Nature to respond
looked up its entry in the votive texts.
It did this to be kind to Rousseauists
who had no time to preen themselves
before ethnology took over. So the wind
joined terror and the regular volunteers.

Chasing a headache down the dam,
closer to Nature than to Real Estate
and picking up the proofs of rational love,
one sprints in darkness through the rushing air
while another clocks the protests
of the telephone. The wind has helped us
draw the face of death. Suppose we had to find
a passage of the Styx—a goat, a pile of coins,
a strangled chook beside—better this wind
than gods about their business. With fingers
in its eyes, it paints itself a holocaust,
back to our dreams, The Wonder Book of Sunsets,
The Raft of the Medusa, a world on fire.

A HEADLAND NEAR ADELAIDE

In this transparency
hung two aviators,
a hang-glider virtuoso
and a little bird,
facing each other
stationary
in the slipping air.

Talk of thermals is no use,
keep your Physics for the blackboard.
The bird was outdaring the man.
The man slithered
and had to right himself
on a jogging current.
The bird edged a little up or down
back to motionless
unblinking confrontation.

This went on quite a time,
evolution slung in space,
the loss so evident
the gain measured only
by the watch upon my wrist.

DIE-BACK

An early choice among the thousand possible
disposables, let me give you an example—
The chuckle of air which flows from a cloud's
occlusion of our only sunny morning of the month;
the loose knob on the door which rattles as
the cat pushes fifty times its weight
across a well-hinged arc; the papers needing tidying
to stop them seeming nests of spite and vanity.
The subject doesn't matter: words are like colours,
they will fit whatever picture's in the making
and it, in turn, this choice of digits on the screen,
is only made to stop a something else
of more intense concern from getting close
to the describable—that's how we move our readers,
we circumvent the masterpiece, we take the weight
off feet by running a funicular to Helicon
with parking space and trolleys and a crèche
for the sublime. How many of you have ever paused
to think of what you owe the suffering artists
of the world? Little by little, as acid eats a plate,
they use up chances and map at least the edges
of the possible, the unendurable. If I know someone
has tamed a bath sponge with a sonnet
I will wash my face today; if my fright at moonlight
has darkened a sestina I might escape insomnia.
Some places are quite exorcized—the foxes in the dripping
    ground,
the thistles on the tongues of Nature Poets.
What's still to do is vast. Each hour a self
is born which may become a juggernaut
no matter how the typhoon lashes at the coasts
of poverty, or new diseases write incipit
on the Immune System.
                    How to spike this bold potential,
this opportunity to make an Enterprise Economy,
is all our skill. The darkness looms: men with ties
adorned with ocelots stand about in suits
at the doors of luxury apartments—this is a Viewing
and the sounds of splashing from the indoor pool
arrive with steam for florid cheeks and collars
till the cheapskate marble weeps—business and desire

outface decay. This unkillable species kills
and goes on being nice to parents, strong on law and order,
its system of despair decked out in hope.
How could our end be uniformly terrible
when our imaginative powers are so confused
we sulk below the level of our fate?
Geniuses may have paid too high a price
for all their optional extras; we do not have the evidence
of their deaths. And information crowds the screen,
a claw-back of the proper passions which should die
but now may live forever. This is the blandishment
of value that our choices are designed to clear,
this electronic smog will activate the systems of despair
until a company secretary screams 'shit'
at a royal visitor, a Chat Show Host hangs himself
ten storeys up, his circuit as he chokes
a half-hour on the clock-face of the dark.

So begins the die-back. The great crowned trees
appear as Light Horse plumes, the branches bare
above the brushed blue tops, a thinning-out
like barbers' rearrangements of the hair
on Managing Directors' scalps. A beetle, a fungus,
a vagrant virus, evolution's other part of the forest,
has changed the whole map of the bush. The cities soak
up soft artesian poisons, the quokkas change their diet
to gleanings from McDonald's, and the desert
seen at night on speculators' charts
scintillates with little spots of death. There will never be
a human spirit equal to the blaze of dying,
no rhetoric to match the chaos in the brain;
but time will save us, ease us to decline
the unsought gift of feeling. As trees gutter to the ground
and alterations to our faces bring on elegy,
we can again dispose of worldliness
by fixing it in a bricolage of words,
our manuscripts left lying on the desk
when wills are read, our mourners struck by visions
we have entertained of nescience,
of lightness once exchanged for consciousness.

A CHAGALL POSTCARD

Is this the nature of all truth,
The blazing cock, the bride aloof,
The E-string cutting like a tooth,
    The night that crows?

The cock has seen the standing grain,
The bride is shrouded by her train,
The violin is strung with pain,
    A cold wind blows.

From earth to sky the cry ascends,
What breaks will threaten where it mends,
Proud lovers end as pallid friends,
    These feed on those.

WHITEBAIT

A multitude of fervours comes to this,
a shoal of silver crispness on a dish:
one man equals ten-thousand fish.

See all the frogs writhing in a pool,
feelings coming in from the cool,
and who'll do it this time, who'll . . . ?

The genocide of creatures which
is the support of life is also life's rich
riot and keeps our howling up to pitch.

CAPITAL AND INTEREST

From the discovery of penicillin
and development of the pill
to the clinical diagnosis of AIDS,
the world had two decades of safe sex.
Such a wicked interregnum
could not go unregarded.
How appropriate, say those
whose highs are power and money,
that we should now be punished
through our sensuality.

But consider it this way.
The human urge to love
can take no stricter path
than through the sexual membranes.
Who then could blame the virus
for crossing to its future
on such a perfect bridge?
A text the New Right might discuss:
market forces pledge success
to the best-equipped contender.

COPYCAT

At least his funeral might be followed
by some of the books he didn't review.

And his notices thrown into the grave,
something to read for a wet eternity.

The stoppage of bells tells that another island
is gone down, the horizon snapping back.

Copycat had grown to love the arbitrary,
maddened by the injustice of good sense.

He'd lived through enskied angelic days
of young Puritans with gourmet needs.

And dons who left their desks on Sundays,
a promise with no need of enemies.

He'd done his best by jokes and syntax
but was a tabby tabbed with unimportance.

His last call to the office asked, could he have
another week, there was still so much to read?

HE WOULD, WOULDN'T HE

He'd say, if pressed, the bomb has kept us free,
We sing the future in an awkward key
But, look, the orthodox revives in me.

As well in acid rain command the tree
To stop its leafing: the moving hands decree
Time has not changed by even one degree.

In whichever place the Emperor chanced to be
The capital was set: the royal we,
Like this man's ukase, came subconsciously.

From Chat Show Host to Superbard we see
The world made new by new ambition, 'The'
(So to say) 'Comedian as the Letter C'.

Apocalypse is followed by High Tea,
Prevailing winds blow fallout out to sea,
The war will make a series for TV.

There still are those who want the CBE.
Bad-tempered diarists praise the Family
And say the Poor live irresponsibly.

Adam, when told by angels that his plea
Had been refused by God, just shrugged like Mandy
And answered, 'Well, He would, wouldn't He.'

SERIOUS DRINKING

It comes from wanting to be perfect.
All human pain from spite to rape
Is just a reading on the grape
And all these living counterfeits
Are for philosophers' defeats;
A discontent so undivine
Moves water one notch up to wine.
Put it away, here comes the prefect.

The sinner is paid in his own coin.
Blood is love's apotheosis
And brings the liver to cirrhosis,
The flowers of sleep which towered stand
Are the famed brandy of the damned
And Wunderkinder who begin
With champagne lights may end in gin.
A drink, lest I forget thee, Zion.

Which human host can match the Devil?
God's watery water is no use—
The anthropologists' excuse
States every known society
Makes alcohol and poetry
Which in their likenesses explore
Creation's toxic metaphor.
Sober I shake and drunk I drivel.

NIGHT WATCH

You sleep less as you grow older
As if it were wiser to stay awake
To be ready for the angel's shake,
The chill of the exposed shoulder.

But it isn't easy to make good use
Of the time you've gained at 3 a.m.
Warm-footed us becomes icy them,
The witty saint the cracked recluse.

To die might be to be fully mad
And sanity to stay open-eyed.
How many of the sane have died
Trying to remember dreams they've had?

TABS ON DICKINSON

Body and Soul drift homeward now
In less than perfect sync,
The Soul which made the longer vow
Impatient of the link.

But none may speed the end of this
Grey firstling of accord—
The Soul is greedy for its bliss,
The Body's seen a sword.

THE FAREWELL STATE

Waking, being glad, not blessing
another day yet taken by surprise
by accustomed miracles, the duvet's
hill of cats, the radio through hiss
coughing fantasies and trivia,
you sense the comfort of your being
momentarily beyond the power
of dreams, their tricks and calms,
extruded on to a world
which feels the cold and sees the point
of cruelty. Remind yourself,
for once, this bourne you live in
owes you nothing—even words and music
float to you from a distant star
whose diligence is unconcerned
with pain or cunning. What then
of wrath and politics at 9,
the shouting and the banging-down
of spoons? The discontent, the poor
gas pressure in the bathroom,
the sky of angled slate beyond
the window—these are commas
of the working day, not needed in
the seamless punctuation
of your dreams, those parables
of Emperor and worm. Make the most
of anger and discomfort then,
and people's grating voices:
tomorrow or some other likely day
the cats will wake and feel they're cold
and seek a warmer contiguity.

SACRED AND PROFANE

They hurry from their storeyed layers
Down to the wet and littered street,
They have not met their far betrayers
But only self and self's defeat.

Nowhere at all is where their home is,
Their greed is small as any mouse
And like a mouse their unfed moan is
Trapped in a dark and shuttered house.

We call apocalypse to flatter
Their pain and say the world's the same,
And yet we know it's no such matter—
Though all must die, not all may blame.

The government of words is vicious
And fills the writer's mouth with gall;
His indignation adventitious,
He is the torturer of all.

THE UNFED APHORISMS

parse this, as boiling water said to steam
trial by train became the fashion-plate

kept up by incompatibility
the weary Devil's nominative muscle

sell a Porsche, be lyrical at last
the consequence of several heavy harvests

wide verandahs magnify the dark
the moon encrusted in the atrium

work had spread to shadeless corridors
vocalize of birds on midday watch

Psyche gives her vote to Cinderella
laburnum transepts cross the tabby's path

to be inscribed on pin-heads: charity
holidays with all the ferries running

corrections in green ink may yet convince
below the salt but still above the mice

after the trepanning homely ghosts
a code is broken in the billiard room

no parking space was left outside Valhalla
their female orphans learned good housekeeping

a friend's polite review is soon outfaced
envy was found more natural than hope

sexual trooping—something from the Raj
gone from the menu, everybody's choice

an ear in your word, the gritty Janus joke
untiring fountains falsify the grounds

ON MALLARMÉ'S ANSWERING MACHINE

Leave the sink to serve the sonnet, Maeve!
After eves of old dove's feathers when
Twilight hangs pegged-out towels and hen
Cries follow, as the bathers leave the wave,

Trudging past your door, you bend
Low, cooking a generation to the grave,
All your elbow's vanity a slave
To these inheritors, your house of men.

This is the call: the saving gesture must
Come from those who clean the moon
With sighs and chamois. Under the dust

A sermon lingers. Put down your cloth
And follow love—who services will soon
Be soft and dressed for dying like a moth.

SUN KING SULKING

In the park the peacocks
have made their own Versailles
but the sparrows prefer a universal slum.

We are classic because we live
so briefly: the ant tells the dung beetle,
'Labour on, Hercules.'

Saint-Simon's entrails exploded
in their funerary bottle—more fun
than the levée of a constipated king.

I said to Molière,
Virtue is above Morality
and my subjects are beneath it.

(I am not usually so easy to follow,
my oracles are toll-gates
and arbitrary confiscations.)

We have always welcomed strangers—
André Breton introducing Henry Miller:
'Gentlemen, the Big Sur Realist.'

Anachronism. I lift my cane
in time with Lully. Elliot Carter
beats down Boulez.

When asked for my reign's greatest
achievement, I've sometimes answered,
M. Perrault's Puss-in-Boots.

Port Royal never interested me
but the cannon-fire at Oudenaarde
made sense of Protestantism.

Dutchmen, Dutchmen, no less,
have resisted my diplomacy,
but I am old, so paint me a victory.

A Mass is worth Paris
as my grandfather didn't say.
He wasn't really an artist.

I recall my chamberlain: 'Sire,
a thousand musicians were born this year
but only one of them is Rameau.'

A fire in the West,
the sun in my window,
I too am a spectacle.

ESSAY ON PATRIOTISM

Compared to my true patriotism,
the imperialism of my legs and bowels,
the suzerainty of my eyes,
grave hemispheric rulings
of the wide Porterian peace,
my love of country is a pallid passion.

So when they say
we've dwindled to a Third Class Power,
a Banana Republic without
a decent satellite to spy from,
I recall those old inheritors
of fear, dirt, snot and rickets
who crawled out of their burrows
to hail Ladysmith's relief
and bray the victories of their rulers
on air they couldn't warm.

Let us therefore handle the word 'great'
with circumspection. It fits Blake
and Milton, is much too big for Cromwell
and generally should watch itself in mirrors,
bearing down like Yeats's Nobel head.

When commentators write about
'the patriotic proletariat',
imagine week-end articles—
'From flat-cap to cat-flap
in one generation', 'Dinkies
are not toys today', 'Designer
Murder comes to Sicily'—
and hang wild garlic round your ears.

Let what people really love
invent an island tongue:
'a gemstone cantilever . . .
hearing it in Noel's SOTA
Dynevector/ Spectral/ Threshold/
Acoustat/ Entec . . .' no wonder
Rambo gobbled up the gooks
if he had such voices in his head.

Patriotism is not enough
of a scoundrel's last refuge
even if you love
your neighbour as yourself.
When I fell from the long tree of light
I didn't know it was going to be me
or I'd have checked all these quotations.
Where I landed I named *ours*
though it was never *mine*.

True patriots all,
the still-swimming lobsters in the tank,
the lambs that face the ocean through steel bars,
the opals in the open-cut—
I left my mother's and my father's house
and stepped on to a road beneath the stars.

AN INGRATE'S ENGLAND

It is too late for denunciation:
That the snow lingers on the sill
And that there are too many newspapers
Is the same as telling yourself
You've given this country forty years
Of your days, you're implicated
In the injustices of pronouns
And the smarter speech of sycamores.

This is the England in your flesh,
A code enduring Summer while
Tasteless birds flap at the edge of
Civilizing concrete. Some have found it
Necessary to reimagine Nature
And stop importing Wordsworth
To shame the bugles from the evening air—
You were born in not the colonies but God.

Yet the brain cannot be Gloucestershire
And vents of human hate are viewed
As old cathedrals across osiers.
The selling of the past to merchants
Of the future is a duty pleasing to
The snarling watercolourist. Prinny
Used to ride by here, and still the smoke
Of loyalist cottages drips acid rain on voices.

The trains in their arched pavilions leave
For restless destinations, their PA Systems
Fastidious with crackle; nobody
Will ask you to identify yourself
But this will lead to hell, the route
The pilgrims take—down the valleys
Of concealed renewal to the pier-theatre,
The crinkle-crankle wall, the graveyard up for sale.

THE CAMERA LOVES US

This is a lucky century, we have more
To leave behind than just our bones.
The minutes of our relaxation
Cry for record, and where a spasm
(Call it hope or pain) might once
have languished just in some sightseer's
Slight recall, we have the lumps of light
To keep it fresh, to turn reflexes
To investments—finally to harrow Hell
With specimens of timeless platitude.

And that is just the start. The camera
Will paint us backwards. More than our
Disappointing mothers it will love us
And groom us into shape. It doesn't merely show
Us to the world but sprays us with its own
Invention till deep-seated ordinariness
Is lacquered by its gleam; the self,
Used to cracking knuckles in dark corners,
Is beamed out as a worldly figurine
Festy with the lens's afterbirth.

It's real, it has been photographed.
The tears aren't sticky but the smile's stuck down.
The soul gets up and leaves this site
And is not missed. Archives are oracles,
No other hell presides beside the grave.
We wonder what the pictures would look like
Were we to see a print of Hadrian
Breakfasting at Tivoli—perhaps
As disappointing as pornography
Where cocksmen camber with their socks on.

The artist came before the camera:
Such fanciful misreading! Walk down
La Rambla past the lines of cages
Filled with doves—do the people eat them, love them?
Or are they what Picasso had to bank
Before he drew his bird of peace? The blood
Runs down the wall, the soldier hurls his rifle
From him as the bullet strikes. People
Are walking to their deaths and will not know
What hits them till the camera christens it.

CIVILIZATION AND ITS DISNEY CONTENTS

Dear Readers, I offer you this impassioned book,
or, should I say, this disquisition on culture
as impassioned as I know how to make it.

It has been so often observed that what we want
is usually to do with food or sex or comfort,
but there are no systems in printing such conclusions.

And systems are what separate us from the animals;
they are the sublimity of our reasoning, the jolt
to eye and brain of the façade of San Miniato.

Our duty is to find them where others see only
a jumble of contrivances, a slogging resonance,
or the dirt-caked misery of the way the world survives.

It will never be forgiven let alone laureated to say
that the trouble with systems is that no one system
can cover everything—to work, a system must be unified.

And so you have before you my Hellenic-Hebraic law,
the tables of which I brought down from the attic,
the universality of family trunks and secrets.

But yet, like a hidden second diary or codicil
to an unfair will, I offer you a few contrary
commonplaces further to my systematic thinking.

We are not put on earth to be happy but to ensure
The effective production of Daihatsu Hatchbacks—
not even the Japanese could want to live in Japan.

Though our lives are short, time is a terrible burden.
Masters think that slavery is necessary to their riches
and slaves know that rich men constitute God's grammar.

You must have met reverent aesthetes patting rarest icons
and have known, while biting on their exquisite food,
their incomes derive from Mail Order jugs of Charles and Di.

Nothing is too far from the grave's edge, or the curtain
slung before the fire. And all the Micky, Dopey, Bambi bits
are to keep your eyes from wandering to the dancing dials.

And yet, why not? To be serious you need a grant
or to have secured tenure. The rest is journalism.
And here's a serious documentary on the survival of the beaver.

At night cicadas mourn the beasts prepared for market.
Tuscan hills vibrate to generators and to rock-and-roll.
The majesty of the Trinity wafts past an old cess-pit.

Bind up the sticks for strength. We are not Fascists.
What will they dig up afterwards of us? Donald Duck is quacking
his charges off to school. He will not tell them he has cancer.

THE POEM TO END POEMS

This poem will get up and off its bed
And let you have the mostly left-out facts,
Such as, it's getting written round about
A theme it's following whose doubtful tracks
Are somewhere in the poet's dusty head:
It fades to life, its past ahead of it.

The theme it's following has special pegs,
Such as, '11 o'clock one day in June,
The trees enleafed, election vans proclaiming
Words as meaningless as opportune,
The mind blocked like a sink and all its dregs
Demanding form but unconcerned with meaning'.

The writer senses that his work must be
Like archaeology on some distant dig
And should he paint the throne-room and declare
It must have looked like that, an endless gig
Of beards and timbrels, bulls and minstrelsy,
He'll turn the serious to the picturesque.

Demanding form but drowning meaning is
The sort of sub-Platonic joking which
An art which flees the sacral is left with:
High Tech should go without a single hitch
And arrogance should never lose its fizz—
You pay the Freudian pension off in myth.

What's new? What's old? What even smells of life?
Today the theorists are the avant-garde,
The artists make it in the Supplements.
The cultural Michelin is stacked and starred
With every genius and his nagging wife—
We keep the templates safe in our bank vaults.

But as I write this down I may uncover
That ring of majesty I know is stored
In words, and by retrieving it I may
Dredge cool reflections from the image-hoard:
Thus while each word remains I will discover
The source from which the magic rays are sent
And publish it this once, the world at play,
Our single sphere which purrs with measurement.

A BUNCH OF FIVES

(*for Kit Wright*)

Caveat emptor! or buyer, be choosy.
Buyer, be choosy and hope to be saved.
Hope, to be saved, must last to the end.
Last to the end is the cringe of the slave.
Cringe, be enslaved, but get your Jacuzzi.

*

Time was the *Greens* were a team
of vicious charioteers. Now the colour
stands for everything the Liberal soul
most desires to save. That whales may roll
through Haydn, the Emperor must dream.

*

Shakespeare on original instruments:
bear-baiters' breath, the Walsingham snivel,
Jack Cade's diphthongs, Douai's Jesuit screams,
boy choristers' simpers, the King's dribble:
an end to RADA decadence.

*

With cognate syntax, you're too far in
already, so Lichtenberg thought.
Every aphorism should abort.
Those are words you're playing around with,
you won't piss wine or grow a fin.

*

The poet Alec Hope has a building
named after him. Birds come to the living
poet's window every day. They grow
accustomed to him. He says, 'I don't know
what they eat, but they'll drink anything.'

*

Rhyme's coming back. Hooray! Hooray!
And stanza and metre and narrative.
Our old hack, metaphor, is blooming,
but under the dressage and the grooming
trot the spavined nags of yesterday.

*

Mallarmé was wrong. Poetry is made
of intervals, the spaces between words.
My Collected Works are all the white
of all the pages I shall ever write,
my First and most victorious Crusade.

*

Here's my crack at Zen. Existence
is the notation of an untranscribable
melody. Art is the incandescence
when you pass the current of the present
through the past's resistance. And then?

*

My mind is like a bookshop chock-a-block
with weighty, plate-filled tomes, all listed as
Porteriana. Customers reconnoitre
for pornography; they loiter,
fingering, not purchasing the stock.

*

Then, as they say, it all became a blur.
I woke in Paradise and it was dark,
I had become my double; there we were,
the carnivore listening to Bach,
the gentle, vegetarian murderer.

*

Why do libraries fill me with unease?
They make me think of God the Great Curator
whose mind stores all atrocities that were
and every death which has yet to occur.
Churches are better, the dead there are at peace.

*

Music begins where words end
(Goethe). But he didn't like the sound
composers added to his words.
His place was on the ground,
the point from which the larks ascend.

*

Planet Earth now boarding through Gate One,
everyone aboard! So these are who
you're flying with, an unimpressive bunch
to find yourself among. Cabin Crew,
doors to manual. The Sun. The Sun.

*

I woke from my dream, crying.
It had been so beautiful,
love personified.
Earlier, I'd woken terrified.
Both dreams had the taste of dying.

*

I stand outside the prodigal's door,
on my own now, my one good angel gone
back to the canton where sun never shone.
O shattering of jugs, O tears unfurled,
I leave the world and am young once more.

LITTLE BUDDHA

'Ich bin der Liebe treuer Stern'

To see its porcelain smile
  Is a surprise in that room
With the electronic junk,
  The albums, the morning gloom,
The empty Pils neatly piled
By the futon, the light sunk
  To a hangover of dreams
  And yet, whatever it seems,
Whether indifferent to
  Fate or expectation or
Luck, its surveillance tells you
  Love can't walk out through the door.

Unbelievers, still stung by
  The need to construct a trust,
Like to set some piece of kitsch
  In place, a Madonna, bust
Of Shakespeare, Sports Day trophy,
Anything numinous which
  Shines in the Humanist dark,
  For they are set to embark
On an unknowable sea
  And the call-sign from afar
In darkness and light is 'I
  Am love's ever-faithful star.'

You sing this and try to prove
  It by rational choosing,
By doing without the bounty
  Of high romantic losing,
Keeping instead to a love
Durable as accounting,
  Traditional as the rhyme's
  Approximated sublime,
And you let the Buddha fix
  On you its unchanging look
Outfacing digital clicks
  And the brandishing of books.

But the warp remains in the soul,
　The obscenity of faith,
The creed that runs in the blood,
　The seventy years of safe
Excess succeeding control,
A dream of desert and flood,
　Of God at the index points
　Whose gift of loving anoints
The numinous animal
　With lyrical avatars,
The lure of impersonal
　Truth, a silence of the stars.

MARKERS

Your death came between Auden's and Britten's
and a few weeks after Connolly's (C.).

The first two you met but hardly knew—
Auden at Heathrow and Britten in Aldeburgh's Post Office.

Connolly you'd seen only on TV
yet you cut his obituary from the paper.

Just as you once cut Randall Swingler's,
a child reaching to the past for an adult's hand.

The long march of the trivial needs markers:
we have to guess if there is terror at the end.

But something tells us to watch the shining
of certain lives as if they were our beacons.

A single plot involves each one of us.
We nestle in the dark against generics.

Then, instead of home and old humiliation,
the starless night of human love appears

And with the great exemplars of our race
we walk out in the cold and pathless air.

OPEN-AIR THEATRE, REGENT'S PARK

In all truth-telling there is waste of art,
Too much of what the soul knows
Can't be said in any working shape
And if an excavation of the heart
Were made for all to see, what grows
Would just disgust and bring no tears.
So I can start sententiously to ape
My feelings, feelings brought about
By words upon a stage. Thirteen years
Since what I hear now was acted there,
The Two Noble Kinsmen, with its plot of rivalry
And the gaoler's randy daughter, out
In the open at Regent's Park, the morris dancers
And the Bavian round and round each bush and tree,
The audience darkening as the lights come on
And you beside me with your groping stare
Trying to fix the limits of despair—
Did Shakespeare write the speech before the goddess?
Auden finds the power of love so strong
It is humiliating, and says Shakespeare loathed
All masculine vanity: I confess
I hear only the multiple inclusive sadness
Of what Human Beings want
Vibrating in the words of Palamon;
I see a dying woman packed with pills
For whom no words would ever be salvation
Yet loyal to the social gestures till
Her heart's punctilio
Faded in mid-sentence. Time comes on
And we won't meet again on this kempt grass.
'Thou that from eleven to ninety reignest
In mortal bosoms, whose chase is this world
And we in herds thy game . . .' of you I ask
The power to disbelieve in you, to protest
At the vicious heraldry which boys and girls
Renew before my eyes, even my own children,
Cavorting along the margins of the grave.
Remake the world so the disappointed live
In a decorum of their usefulness,
Intervene in theatres of despair to save
The humorous and timid—it was your altar

Which we visited one bad summer in the park
Because we thought Shakespeare's hand was there
And liked collecting rarely-given plays,
And sucked from you the poison of your art
And heard your words die in the timid greys
Of what was green with love before the start.

THEY COME BACK MORE

And I thought they all had gone. Through doors
They hardly knew were there, the sick bays
With their yellow curtains or into legends
Of hard starts in life, of families losing fortunes
And long years of night school, the maimed and poisoned
Ancestors who take the place of history
And Marxist arbitration. And take the place of love
So that my life has been a pilgrimage
To safe refinement, the arch and etching of the cry
And not the cry itself. Where I should have packed
My sandshoes, taken a striped towel and zinc cream
To the sun, I sulked instead of Genoa velvet
For Old Vienna and old manses. Now I see the outcome;
These ghosts are as rich in real estate in heaven
As they were in Surfers Paradise; they have endowed
The trees; the city takes its pallor from their smiles,
My father the only spirit exiled from
A world he couldn't hate. The fire of his death
Became the Queensland sun; he's trapped in me
And I would wish him sky's forgetfulness.

And he's first back, in braces over flannelette,
Boiling cigar butts in a saucepan, planning
A lethal spray for aphis. Details for my mother
Are a harder bet, and betting was her florid best,
Having dreamed a winner in the darkest welter
Of her flesh—always willing to concede
That Eden had a tradesmen's entrance, she
Passed to death from exile, fearing both.
Yet she's the spirit of all cake-baking,
Laughter, kitchen-prowess, which inheritance
Proved to be a love of art: she may have thought
Mozart the favourite for the Seven Furlongs
But she knew instinctively our brains
Must be as intricate and wonderful a score
As anything he wrote if his great pattern
Should delight us. However she appears, in tan
Shoes and white-brimmed hat, or flaming
Pubicly from an afternoon hot-bath,
She and I will recognize each other,
The playful faces in the scowling crowd.

And such strange friends return, so say hello
To the iceland poppies and the zinnias,
The male and female pawpaws and the passion-fruit,
Straggling a drop of sixteen feet from our
Back landing to the wash-house and its copper—
Between this underworld of stumps and palings
And the long back hedge of bougainvillea
Was where I filtered Europe through Australia:
Renunculus and asters loved to learn
The Magic Flute and William Walton
And cared for Ansons more than Wirraways—
It helped them to endure the Brisbane heat
While my father scanned the wasps and buzzed about
The garden scolding Natives, emptying
Love on his more brittle blooms. If 'under-the-house'
Was sex and guilt, the garden was salt Paradise,
The field of art. I knew to an instant's blick
I came from nowhere but had somewhere dire
To go, that we are granted lease of sun
And sounds of water to console us here,
An interregnum in the war of flesh
When Caliban and God sunbathe together.

And a tousled sunburst opens up to haunt
The daylight's overdream, an impromptu ballet
Of things which live because their owner died.
That bag with green and orange leather patches,
Gawky handles and a hardihood of hessian,
Bought beside the Vatican walls before
A morning gin blurred judgement—it went, I think,
To LA to outlive another's death;
The mirror ormolu'd to seem as if
Someone had been robbing Shaftesbury Avenue,
Preserving guilty looks no matter how
Clear the conscience of the glass—and will it show
Her face in Heaven? The plain watch on my wrist,
Repeating its warning of the end of things
Though it only winds and isn't digital—
It was her gift and keeps near-perfect time,
A calibrator of the perished hours
When hurt and humour raced us to the dark.
She's not come back but sends her artefacts
To represent her; nothing wipes the pain
From dusty surfaces, and as I list

The souls of these inanimates I know
They'll turn to flesh in death and guide me to
A warehouse of unclaimed identity.

And they come back more, the more to kill.
Till now my own dead body would have been
The first corpse I had seen but here these close
Ur-Revenants and friends are sent to shroud
Me with their occult shadows, to lounge about
As half-official yuppie psychopomps.
The traps are laid by language, the Judge's jokes
Hang everyone; our ducts of sense are zones
Of Eros, himself a god who forged his past.
They come back more, hoping to appear
On diary pages not to be indexed;
They know the world to be intrinsically
Evil, that whatever sense we make of time
To write *Finis Coronat Opus* will be
Some sort of privilege, and nobody is waiting
To meet us when we land. They will not live
As shades but angle forward to enjoy
The pluck of life, the pressure of their ichor.
And to resume? To live again, to stare
At eyes which happily occluded light
And pain of light? This must be banishment
And must be what the dream is dressing in,
The joining of our hands, the ampersand.

And the axiom asks always to be proved.

FROGS OUTSIDE BARBISCHIO

How reassuring to listen to frogs once more
From stagnant water in an old brick cistern
Beside olive trees run wild and the unprogrammed
Flight of a butterfly over hot fields and terraces.
One grandfather frog stays on his stick to watch
A self-tormentor return to his book to trace
His anatomy of melancholy. He's in Italy
To surprise an old hopelessness known long before.

The cosmos of frogs inside its wet-walled fort
Warbles and cavorts in the all that there is.
Wise frog rejoinders have challenged that book:
Come down to our waters so pulsingly black
And lose all your stubble of fortune and truth.
Here's art inside art, incision and sign
Of the purposeless minute outlasting its span,
Of the gloat and the plop and the stick still afloat.

PORTER'S RETREAT

Once the difficulty had been
to cross the Divide, to follow spurs
which seemed to end in air,
to swivel about the cobwebs where the creeks
dipped below their spiders to
a contrary encircling of your steps—
to keep on through the undergrowth
with only stripes of sun above,
to get beyond these endless-seeming vistas
and look out on the plain which might contain
a sea, a minareted island, a mirage,
whose common epithet was Felix,
appointed place of all felicity.

There are, of course, bland natures
back at home, whose only earnest
is a theory that your expedition
means to straighten out the land with names,
to fit a grid of the accounting gods
on plastic otherness. You'll have to give
a hostage to them—do it now.
Here by Disappointment Bluff, gaze
across the Vale of Sixty to Uncanniness;
beyond the rock-strewn creek
is an escarpment called Incalculable
and the fields are more elided than Elysian—
mark this tree the point of going back
and set it on the map—Porter's Retreat—
the place at which all further progress
ceases to have consequence.

But expeditions never go as planned.
You're given a foretaste of the future:
a set of barbecue emplacements,
Olympic Pool, koala sanctuary,
suggestions for a heliport—
journeys inland have moved Nature
from the coast: this is the people's fort
where families collaborate with the sun
to make home-movies of divinity.

You're far beyond here now,
digging for nurture under balding trees,
only too willing to fold up the map
and start the evening's diary entry—
tomorrow will be another scorcher,
meanwhile this heap of gutted granite
shall be named Mt Misery
and the muddy tank-full where the river
dips into the underworld will make
a just impression as Lake Longevity.

MUSICAL MURDERS

Tromboncino and Gesualdo,
two composers killed their wives.

Their temperaments were 'molto caldo',
Tromboncino and Gesualdo.

From Sabbionetta to Certaldo
sung notes were not as sharp as knives.

Tromboncino and Gesualdo,
composers who killed faithless wives.

*

Two others were stabbed in the street,
Stradella and J. M. Leclair.

Their lives and loves were indiscreet,
these others murdered in the street.

For journeys end when lovers meet
a jealous step upon the stair.

Composers murdered in the street,
Stradella and J. M. Leclair.

THE ORCHARD IN E-FLAT

The waves are weeping vaguely. Confessional dust
Plagues the opacity of ocean and a book
Lies down at angles—scene-setting by our sons.
A god is rising from the ambient air
As though there were no griefs and nothing died
But there appeared a wholesome vanity
For us to live in: evangelizing light
Is spread before a holy picnic, goats
And men move down the isthmus to dark bells.

The numberlessness of stones is speaking for
The helplessness of people—debts, deaths and
Spoliations are a tuning of the world,
A chord of limitless additions, but
Anywhere a road leads over hills
And temperate dawns to some encumbered cabin
Where the bruise of exile turns to timeless rose.

Sequences are set by leaves, the ripplers' coven,
Even as Aeolian sounds are congregated
To pick up yells of history or the bubble-breath
Of dying, separate conveyances of truth,
Some convected into keyboard plausibilities
And some to concert strokes of sanity.
Evil at its console feels for carpet-slippers
Choosing the classiness of the baroque.
Surely such categories include the double.

Behind us is the deep note of the universe,
The E-Flat pedal on which time is built,
Spreading and changing, both a subtle
Growth of difference and a minimalist
Phrase, with bridges crossing it and staves
Of traffic on its tide, a broad bloodstream
To carry to the delta full mythologies.

A mother and a boy come to the orchard
To turn a cow back to its field; they see
The ducks in line-ahead among the crimson
Pointillism of the windfalls and,

Overheard by them, the everlasting anthem
Changes as injustice starts to sing—
There's wood enough within: it fires the earth,
The creatures coming home, the buried bones
And pairs of ears poised, the weeping waves.

STRATAGEMS OF THE SPIRIT

You've reckoned without the world. The soil
Itself is pure sententiousness, the ocean
Argues with it when the wind springs up
And corpses won't stay buried. So many saints
Are unemployed, they can't turn down a part
Even if it's no better than a minor role
In some low-budget Tempting—feasting
Out of bounds or tripping up a donkey
In a culver, raising billhooks from lake bottoms.
The artist praises God according to
His pattern book; it's wholly orthodox
And worth his modest fee—but look aside,
He's really interested in something else:
A young girl pouring milk, a skiff the wind's struck
Going about. That's his Te Deum, rushes
In the evening swaying to the shore. We're so far
Into history, we relish the cordon bleu
Of abstinence, our stomachs and our bowels
Are training for the confidence of stones—
All this continues years beyond the Age
Of Faith: we just have uglier pictures now,
Paler credulities: the earth will not
Co-operate but sulks inside its tent
Of miracles. And we must watch our crude
Interpreters muddy up the halcyon—
If the slit in the Madonna's dress
Is sexual and she fingers it, the tent
Above her like a conquering glans, it's God
Day-dreaming a new gender for the war
In Heaven: a marvellous smile which runs
Through flesh *del parto*, headlong on to love.
Think too of angels which no man but Blake
Has ever seen—yet how everyday and picknicky
They look just holding back the curtaining,
How like the cousins you'd have liked to have.
They could be Stevens's invisibles,
They wouldn't need to borrow trumpets in
A land of intervention—might they be
The plot, the shining embryo, the blot
Of Jesus on his mother? It's too late
To be religious in the census sense,

The sons of Benedict have so baptised
The landscape, it's all hungry soul—No,
The spirit's excellent stratagems are set
To bring on other platitudes: we
Must think ourselves alive and newly-landed,
Star-faced Linneans hearing musical
Communiqués no erudition robs
Of freshness—we must pace our footfall on
The temple steps and listen for the sun.

HAND IN HAND

They are always together, the two who travel
But never know when they must separate,
A gravely frowning pair in gloaming who
Cast such savage shadows that the beasts
Stir in their tiers (sweet macaronic pun)
At this invisible portage, that the rivers
Etch their banks to fine-drawn lines
And music forms a gum upon the air.
They are hand in hand; no looking-back
Is necessary, but their fear is palpable—
Their Hermes is a harvest of remembering
As if they had been born to gather in
A future lived already: it must be this
Since tiredness was their starting-point
And faith like sunlight faded in betrayal.
The onwardness is strange; they grow old
But won't believe in time; they are fed on words
And every disappearing trick; an abbey
Is a schoolyard and a paysage
With carrion birds reveals its toothy fright
In pictures of a mother. By interchangeability
The world subsides to sex, its surfaces
All lust, its membrane's history's odd halves.
That hand's in this hand, so no one sees
Their partnership is change, that love is like
A signal passing which may startle air
Only by its afterglow: is this a death,
Not of the one or other but of all?
Huge horns stake the mountains in their places,
A damning rung of darkness widening
Until the sea itself withdraws to show
The puny two still wearing eyes like hats.
One hand undid the swaddling wraps of pain,
The next one vanished in a coffin's echoings,
And yet one further bent down further to
Raise love to love, hydraulic vanity;
The last hand and the best enskies the heart
Along this path grown Mannerist where gods
Quote from their memories. Dark and darkening
Are the Furies' tails, whip-lashing light
On snow-tiled Erebus. Avert the eyes

And do not glance aside to question who
Is there. The species is the soul on trial,
Its pilgrimage a handclasp from despair,
Walking with Hermes to the upper air.

TALKING TO THE LIZARDS

It's true. Nobody should live all his time here, away from the dust
    Of delivery vehicles, away from
The knowledge that news is arriving which turns men's complexions
    to
        Maps, tells them that labour's relentless as life,
With queues of fine spirits sold up for breaking. The city is there
    At the end of all roads; may it forget me
If I forget it. I won't even tickle a letter, watching
    The lake, or savage the swans' punctuation—
Instead I'll endure the bad prose of the insects, their redundant
    Lyrics. Dance early death, life is escaping.
You wouldn't expect this: Cicero, master of morals, his grim
    Jar of precedents shut, sitting in sunshine:
The songs of first days are as sweet as smoked honey, the hazes of
    Noon in a month without rain—the upside-down
Landscape says walk on the air, this dust is from planets as lucky
    As Caesar. Thus we deceive ourselves, country-
wise, country-slow, stooping to scratch the hog marked for
    slaughter, his snout
        In petunias. My books are my truffles,
I dig them in dreams. Last night when mosquitoes like bores in the
    Senate
        Sang me to sleep, I saw a face open which
Had been a Roman's, a hard politician's whose love was on sale,
    Whose words were like nightmares where lampposts become
Portable gibbets—this gruesome effigy was too everyday
    To terrify me: a waking disturbance
Rocked me instead—a drunk screaming death at policemen and
    tourists—
        They dragged him away but from his foul frothing
Caesar's great conquests appeared like prisons, the world he is
    making
        To lock us all in. Hate is a flag which flies
Above rulers: they know our weakness, our envies and spitefulness;
    The sum of our decency to them is mere
Anarchy, the state falling apart in kindness and service. I
    Fear that the gods are awake after sleeping
And mean to be noticed: the Innocent Age has slunk to its cave,
    The Epoch of Turbulence waits at the rim.
On nights when the moon is a sliver I shudder to see beyond
    Darkness the countryside's monster uprooting

The farms, the roads and the vineyards—the spirit of timeliness
　　Washing in blood. I wait then for morning to
Show me the lizards convecting the flagstones, a sensitive
　　Ballet of substance and shadow, the spring
Of their probing convulsed beyond truculence. A politician
　　Should study lizards; their ludic rehearsal
Will clear his head and then when he sits at his desk again writing
　　He'll think of their dart and release, their having
No path to prepare. He'll say to himself, We make music when we
　　Act, almost as beautiful as real music,
A patterned disinterest like the movement of limbs across marble.

COPYRIGHT UNIVERSAL PICTURES

An immensely gifted palaeontologist
Shard-sifter has brought his virtuoso
Teenage viola-playing daughter
To the island to join him on the dig
And so encourage her to forget the quite
Unsuitable roller-skating son of a rabbi
Now proprietor of a pineapple cannery
On a remote bayou in Cajun country.

She has already noticed the only brother
Of the schizoid Alexandrian owner
Of the Crusader Castle where they excavate
Mosaics of Pyramus and Thisbe and airbcine
Ganymede, the oldest of their kind in Paphos.
He has published one book of sonnets privately
From Keele University entitled *Atlantis, Atys,
Attica*, and brought his Burt Reynolds videos.

Professor Fuori Sanguinetti, who has had to leave
Catania University hurriedly and who hopes to
Acquire some Hellenistic artefacts for a firm
Of antiquarians in the Veneto to whom his wife
Is seriously in debt, suspects that our
Loving father is not everything he seems and that
The Manager of the Phylloxenia Hotel
Is either an agent of the KGB or CIA or both.

The poet is on a deserted beach breaking open
Shells for the viola-player, telling her how the fish
When boiled made a purple dye called Murex—
'Gee, you're a bore,' she says. 'I came here to get laid.'
The little waves like Aphrodite's feet lie down
In the spume and gulls snatch wrappers from the sand—
This is the scene she said she wouldn't do nude
Which will be on the posters when the film's released.

The Professor has followed them and watches from
The dunes; above the bay a helicopter circles
While a fishing boat is anchored out of sight
Below the Rock of All the Romans. Along the road

The Manager approaches in a Pre-War Chev.
We are not shown what will become of this
And pan back to the diggings where we see
The child-god simper in the eagle's claws.

The poet has begun a sonnet and from a room
Just over his the sound of Paganini studies
Drives an alto nimbus through the evening light;
Reynolds has beaten up a man in an all-night
Diner in St Louis, and the screen goes blank—
The girl and her father come into the lobby and greet
A man in a panama hat whose sweat-circles
Below his arms spread almost to his waist.

Articles of clothing catch the moon beside
The hotel swimming pool. Arpeggios of bubbles
Accompany naked limbs. A blue fish from Murano
Swims in air above Reception and trunks are loaded
On a BMW. The story will move on to Rhodes
And leave this cheap-to-film-in corner
Of the great inane. Leave, too, the unimportant
Like ourselves. Next shift, it may be Athens.

THE NEW MANDEVILLE

I

The people of this place are activists
Of the spirit's incompleteness, living
In expatriation from death, a state
Always anticipated, never known,
And so they place their clocks on traffic-lights
To tell the time of immanence. Missing death
Their value models are phenomena
And pictures borrowed from their neighbour state,
The Adversarial Isles. Decorum and good taste
Are taught by Masters of Imagination,
Proposing such Last Things as rage in orchards
After hailstorms, or Trecento altarpieces
Abandoned in some distant gravel-yard.
If we could die we could have history,
That rosy cause of all exhaustion,
Plus multi-layered books to write it in,
They like to think. Their exports are their mirrors
Which reflect the soul and not the expected face,
Very attractive to the vainer peoples,
But their afternoons are stunned and effortful
With everything from sex to conveyancing
Confined to morning hours. Missionaries
Have laughed to say the only beads attractive
To them are the rosary and that
A pear-shaped mole of orange hue found on
Their faces has been named 'The Lacrymosa'.
These then are people who define themselves
By one great missingness undoing all
Which love and speculation should insure.
The change they never fail to pray will come
May yet be drawing closer: not a wind
Like whiteness from the East waking disease,
Nor some Messiah raised on ruby yoghurt
Setting out to cross the tall Sierras
To an entrepôt, but economic shifts
Which foil both Planners and Free Marketeers—
So many have gone missing in between
Two latitudes of one peninsula
They coin the phrase 'Consumer Triangle'
And warn the esoteric seekers-out

63

Of ploys to counter boredom that a false
Connection with mortality is worse
Than floating down eternal afternoon,
So they should keep their patience for their sleep
And dream an intimation of an end.

2

Our captain entertained us with tales
Of haunted floatings, of the *Marie*
Celeste and drifting Zeppelins with meals
      Still hot on tables.

Good preparation for our landfall,
The twilight archipelago named
Archivia. The mist here is dense
      With unstopped music.

A land without population but
Rich in society: pictures
Freed from Museums posing beside
      Their unpainted selves,

Books, as punctual as newspapers,
Sitting at tables over Happy
Hour, swapping paricides and dram-
      atis personae.

Tantrums here are tantric—watch a note
Cut from its tonic contemplate some
Passage into joy to change the course
      of modulation.

This world, so beautifully inscribed,
So underpinned by scrupulous pain,
So ruled by registers of others,
      Will last forever.

And has, the records show, outfaced its threats:
The Deconstructors' Insurrection,
The Death of Summary, then Silence,
      Exile and Cunning.

It's always Conference Time. Hotels
Advertise such comforts as 'Bring your
Own Death' and 'Permutate confession
        In our dream language.'

Tonight they're playing 'Exit, Pursued
By a Bard' and 'The Passion According
To St Bach', but jokes are seriatim's
        Ectoplasmic end.

Visit the Museum of the Future,
Goggle at the Dance of the Unborn
Masterpieces, try to imagine
        Living in a world

Where Sviatoslav Bimbo never
Existed, where the triptych 'The Mass
At the Trocadéro' wasn't hung
        And Brut was only

An aftershave. Prayer-wheels turning fly
The flag of ecstasy, The Serious
Squad arrests a frivolous graffitist
        Caught in the act of

Spraying 'Penis Angelicus' on
The windows of a music store. Time
Is the supreme swear-word, the last
        Emancipation.

The Mega-Store of Harmony stays
Open every night to harness
Exclamations of the million words
        That triumph trod on.

Each watering-place and Crossroads Cap-
ital affords a Festival: 'The
Parleying of Photographs', 'Redan
        of Recusancy',

'Salon des Diffusés'—the racks of
MIMs* are raised to light from underground,
A Demo-Pantheon assuring
      Immortality

Its quarter of an hour. Ice-cream
Emperors, seconded to the parks
And crematoria, lend leaves their
      Best metonymy.

We tourists feel forlorn as if we'd
Lacked a chapter heading at our birth
Or got through childhood glued to the box
      With no memories

Of Sunday School or nominating
'Black Beauty' as a prize. Yet there are
Copious compensations: Book Wars
      On the Bioscope,

The trenches winding through Arcadia,
The Glossary Grand Tour, and for the up-
to-date a kinesthetic keyboard with
      Finger-tip control

Of metaphor, a sort of 'Chips with
Everyman'. The afternoons are hung
With sentences which Sterne bequeathed to
      Universities.

The elaborations last. The lion
Lies down with the lamb, desire spins its
Cool cocoon and love is free to love
      Itself as syntax.

          * 'Mute Inglorious Miltons'

66

After the Tableland of Dreams our next
Intention was to kick the switchback to
High End, that showland, ever-changing Expo
Of the newest redeployments of the Spirit
Where greedy fables are precisely nimble
Whichever laser-digits phrase the murk
Of history—instead a fever took
Our bodies to a very different place,
A veiled occluded territory
Haunted by a tribe of disparates,
A sort of deep defile like Syracuse's
Quarry prison. To some its title is
'The Swamp of Suicides', to others 'New
Samaria'—patterned like a hand
Which clenches and unclenches constantly.
Its calm is voices ceasing, and its hope
A closure of all doors, its air-free sounds
Proclaim there are no questions here, the end
Of ending is so beautiful. This lie,
Consistent with each other lie, permits
The pain of stopping to persist as pain,
The images of human unredemption
To come back as 'The Generation Show',
With teenage fury always at rewind
And envy cataloguing its CDs.
The true books came as liberators, they
Reproduced the best historic hells,
The Lagers, Genocides, Apostalates,
But nothing here would print such images,
Their documentaries faded when the self
Looked from its attic to the childhood lawn
And saw its shape, the grass beneath the blade.
A nation whose last words are not to be
Esteemed makes this its only poetry:
'I die' (iambic), 'death comes' (trochee), 'dead
As dust' (dactylic), 'Thou shalt die' (an
Anapaest), 'Proud Death' (the spondee)—hearts
As much as God are spiked on prosody,
The silent voices chant and are not heard.

And then we set out from this backward Cave
Of Cadences to rejoin the world and felt
The breeze of commerce moving on our faces,
The sun re-focus on our skin, and birds,
Which had been idling in our wake, construct
A future round our ears with fervent cries.

OXFORD POETS

Fleur Adcock
James Berry
Edward Kamau Brathwaite
Joseph Brodsky
Michael Donaghy
D. J. Enright
Roy Fisher
David Gascoyne
David Harsent
Anthony Hecht
Zbigniew Herbert
Thomas Kinsella
Brad Leithauser
Derek Mahon
Medbh McGuckian
James Merrill

John Montague
Peter Porter
Craig Raine
Christopher Reid
Stephen Romer
Carole Satyamurti
Peter Scupham
Penelope Shuttle
Louis Simpson
Anne Stevenson
George Szirtes
Grete Tartler
Charles Tomlinson
Chris Wallace-Crabbe
Hugo Williams

also

Basil Bunting
W. H. Davies
Keith Douglas
Ivor Gurney
Edward Thomas